Grandpa School

Matthew Cramer

Library of Congress Control Number: 2018945376

ISBN 9780983979463

Design and illustration by
Richard Schletty
schlettydesign.com

Published by:
The Cramer Institute of Minnnesota
Lakeville, MN 55044
www.cramer-institute.com

DEDICATION

For my daughter,

Cheryl Ann.

She never gives up.

CHAPTER LIST

Introduction 1

About God. 3

Who Am I? 9

Evil and Redemption. 15

The Bible. 21

Religion. 25

Discernment 31

Emotions, Sex, and The Mind 37

Love and Dating. 43

Marriage 51

A Man of God 57

PREFACE

Too many years ago, our eight grandchildren were in different degrees of teenage. Their parents led very busy lives, and I grew concerned about their preparation for the vicissitudes of life.

My parents were divorced; my father was absent. I received little, if any, mentoring about emotions, the demands of religion, dating, relationships, and so on. I played maturity catch-up most of my life, and it was a struggle. I would have given a small fortune to be mentored into adulthood.

Our grandchildren consisted of six boys and two girls. Their parents were fully capable of raising their sons and daughters properly and in love, but I wanted to make sure I got my two cents in.

So I called my idea Grandpa School, and asked them to meet with me for two or three sessions. My wife, Ruth Ann, handled the girls. We talked, straight up, about life: God, church, dating, emotions, sex, and so on.

At first, there was wasn't much discussion, but they began sharing tidbits with their friends. At some point, they invited a friend or two to join us, then mothers began asking for their sons to attend.

Grandpa School continued with several sessions every year depending on the subject matter. It ended after three years when I'd finished my say.

My daughter has frequently urged me to commit Grandpa School to writing. I now have seven great-grandchildren who are growing up like weeds, as they do. The eldest is thirteen.

Thus, I present herein my best recollection of Grandpa School; salted, of course, with the fruit of my successes and failures in the twenty years since.

This book is written as a primer for a parent or grandparent who wants to discuss these subjects with their progeny, as I did. I make no claim that I've covered in depth all of the life's issues, just a few points I think are important.

For the sake of simplicity, the material is presented in a straight forward fashion with little nuancing or expansion for context. I've assumed sufficient amplification and explanation will be provided by a session leader.

The chapters are mostly self-contained, so they can be discussed out of sequence.

From this point forward, the text is written as a parent or grandparent addressing their offspring. Biblical translation acronyms continue in order without notation after the first one, until changed by a different one, and so on. The acronyms are:

CCC	Catechism of the Catholic Church
KJV	King James Version
NRSV	New Revised Standard Version
NRSVCE	New Revised Standard Version Catholic Edition
RSV	Revised Standard Version

Introduction

In Grandpa School we'll talk about God, offer some proof that he's real—with a little bit of theology—reveal how much he loves you, and talk about his requirements and strategies for you to lead a successful life.

The most important question you'll ever get in life is: What are you going to do about God? Your answer and how you live it, will be life changing. The question will come up over and over because life requires difficult decisions that have far-reaching effects.

There are many answers to this question, but the best one is: develop a relationship with God and stick with it. To do that, you must believe he is available to you. He's a God of love; you can talk with him, complain, ask for help and get answers. He's your friend, your protector, and your guide in life.

Many people believe in God, but they think he stands way off in Heaven, makes a lot of rules, and sits in judgment when you die. But that's not correct.

Yes, God has some rules to help us stay close to him. But, we'll see how God is constantly involved in your life, from the very beginning to the end. He created you to live with him, and he sacrificed his only Son on a cross so you could achieve your intended destiny.

We'll talk here in some detail about a few of life's issues. You might learn a couple of new words. But don't ever forget that God is real, a personal God of love. He loves you, and he is available to you 24/7.

For simplicity, the words *man*, *he*, and *him* herein are intended to mean both the male and female variety.

About God

Creation's How

When you take in the view around you—the beauty, complexity, and order in nature and the universe—do you wonder who started all this?

For centuries, people have struggled with this question. Those who believe in God assert that you were uniquely created to live with him in Heaven, and you must choose to do so by obeying him in your life.

There are those who do not believe. They claim God is a myth, a story developed by unsophisticated people who did not have the technical smarts to understand life and creation. By eliminating God, they feel free to ignore his rules; unless it suits them to comply.

Scientists have been studying HOW creation got started, and they're making progress. But all of their technology and studies have never moved us an inch toward WHO started all this.

The latest wisdom of science tells us how creation happened in the big bang theory. In the beginning, there was nothing. Then there was a big bang, and all of the elements required for what we see today were spun out into the universe.

But it's still a theory. Science has a lot of theories. It's the way they do business. But scientific theories must be proved before being accepted as fact.

The big bang theory is popular today, but it only talks about HOW creation could have happened. And it's missing two answers: Where did the stuff that got banged come from? Who did the banging?

So, let's leave the HOW of creation to the scientists, and talk about the WHO.

Prime Mover

Some people say that creation just evolved over time from some elementary matter. But if you trace backward from anything, asking each time: "Where did that come from?" eventually, you run out of answers. You reach a point where something had to come from nothing.

But how can that be? Everything that exists can be traced to something it came from. Science tells us that. The answer is: There must be someone or something that always existed, a *being* (creator) who is the primary source of all that exists in creation. Such a *being* is often called the Prime Mover.

The creator being must have existed all by himself, with no beginning or end. He just is. We use the mathematical term *infinite* to mean no limits. Whoever started creation had nothing to work with except himself. He had to be infinitely smart and infinitely powerful to get the job done from nothing. So, we call the creator an infinite, spiritual *being*.

If I say: "What are you?" your answer would be: "I am a human *being*." Human *beings* are a higher order in creation, having a body, a soul, an intellect, and a will. They can know things, decide things, and act on them. Rocks, trees, animals, fish, insects, and snakes cannot.

Whenever we say WHO, we mean a person. A person is a *being* who can think and act. If I say: "Who are you?" your answer might be, "I am Sheldon Cravitz. I play guitar, and I don't do well in math." You are a person, unique among many human beings.

Notice the distinction between the WHAT and the WHO. WHAT refers to the state of your *being,* the kind of *being* you are. WHO refers to your individual character and decisions.

God's What and Who

The name given the Prime Mover, the Creator *being*, is God. So, let's start with his WHAT:

- He is the one and only infinite being—the Prime Mover, the Source of existence, without beginning or end.
- He is infinitely smart and powerful, without limits, incapable of error.
- He is a spiritual being, unconstrained by time or flesh.
- He is a person, able to think and act.

Now let's talk about his WHO:

- He is the Creator.
- All of the goodness we encounter is present in him.
- Most important of these is love: He has a godly love, willing to sacrifice his own person for the needs of his beloved.
- Other good things about God are: mercy, justice, forgiveness, long-suffering, etc. The complete list is very long.
- He's a *person* of infinite, perfect love and goodness; there can be no place in his presence for non-good things, like hate, guilt, fear, envy, and all of the other evils.

Revelation

But there is another way we can know God exists, his WHO and WHAT. He's told us himself. It's all recorded in the Bible.

Some people think of the Bible as quaint stories, anecdotes and myths. Still, the Bible has been accepted by Christians as a trustworthy source of truth about spiritual matters for more than two thousand years.

God has made himself known in many ways since mankind began. Those visitations were mostly specific instructions. People knew there must be a God, but had no idea who or what he was, or if there was one or many. So, they invented gods, gave them names, personalities, and stories.

The Jewish people have long had a special relationship with God. In the biblical year 2000 BC (before Christ), God told a man named Abraham to leave what is now Iraq, travel west to a promised land, what is now Israel, and start a new nation. They were to be God's people. Thus, the Jews are called "the Chosen People."

Five hundred years later, around 1500 BC, the descendants of Abraham, the Jewish people, called Israelites at the time, were enslaved in Egypt. God appeared in a burning bush to a Jew named Moses, identified himself as God—"I AM WHO AM" (Ex 3:14 NRSVCE)—and told Moses to lead the Israelites back to Israel.

To say "I am" indicates a person who can think and act. "Who am" means a *being* outside of time, a being who just *is*; no beginning, no end—no limits. Infinite. We've already seen earlier what that means.

During the exodus from Egypt, God gave Moses Ten Commandments containing rules he wants the Chosen People to follow. For the next 1,500 years, the Chosen People followed their one and only God through many wars and persecutions. Jews and Christians still follow these rules today.

Three Persons, One God

Around 3 BC, a Jew named Jesus was born, and began his ministry some thirty years later. He said he was the Son of God, and promised to send a third person from God, called the Holy Spirit, to help his followers live their lives.

All of this shocked the Jews. There can be only one God. How can there be three?

But Jesus backed up his claim with many miracles and predicted he would rise from the dead. He claimed to be one with the Father in the same *being*. But he also claimed to be a separate *person* in the Godhead. To the Jews, such a thought was blasphemy, against 1,500 years of tradition, and it led, in part, to Jesus' crucifixion.

Jesus did rise from the dead and ascend into Heaven. The Holy Spirit descended on the apostles at Pentecost and remains with us to this day.

Today, Christians are followers of Jesus Christ. Our faith is rooted in the Jewish faith. But we believe that God is one, infinite *Being*, shared with three separate *persons*: Father, Son, and Holy Spirit.

Understanding the WHO and WHAT of God encourages faith in us that he is real and loves us. I've learned that an ongoing relationship with God is the bedrock of a happy and successful life. I recommend one for you.

Who Am I?

God is the Creator; an infinitely smart and powerful spiritual *Being*; a God of infinite love; one *Being*, three persons—Father, Son, and Holy Spirit.

A very important word and concept must now be introduced—it's called *rectitude* (rek-ti-tood). It means the proper purpose and function for something, defined by a superior being. Rocks do rock things, dogs do dog things, trees do tree things. Their rectitude is obvious in nature.

When God creates something, he defines its rectitude, along with its mission and operating instructions. You are a human *being*. Your life, your creation, gives you an opportunity to live with God in Heaven. But, God requires you to think and act in a manner consistent with your rectitude.

You are granted free will to follow or reject your rectitude, God's creation in you. You are not a puppet. But if you want to succeed in life, and live with God in Heaven, you must be faithful to the creation he has installed in you.

Mankind

You are a human *being*, part of a larger group named mankind, humanity, or as in the Bible, just man.

Mankind has a physical body and a soul. The soul is a free-willed spirit that installs the intellect, the will, and the gift of life. It acts through the body and can receive spiritual input. As conception occurs, the soul enlivens the body; they are thoroughly integrated and act as one being in all things.

> Then God said, "Let us make man in our image, after our likeness..." So God created man in his own image, in the image of God he created him; male and female he created them" (Gen 1:26-27 RSVCE).

Over 4,000 years before Christ, God created man as a person like himself—alive, with an intellect, and a will—free to act as he decides. Obviously, we're missing the infinite part. The first man was Adam.

Eve, the first woman, was created to be a partner with Adam. She was formed from him, and her rectitude is the same as Adam's.

> So the LORD God caused a deep sleep to fall upon the man, and while he slept took one of his ribs... and made [it] into a woman and brought her to the man. Then the man said, "This at last is bone of my bones and flesh of my flesh; she shall be called Woman, because she was taken out of Man" (Gen 2:21-23). (Some think a modern translation might be: "Whoa, God, you rock!")

The woman and man are equal partners, responsible to each other in pursuit of their mission and creating new life with God.

> And God blessed them, and God said to them, "Be fruitful and multiply, and fill the earth and subdue it; and have dominion over... every living thing that moves upon the earth." Therefore a man leaves his father and his mother and cleaves to his wife, and they become one flesh (Gen 1:28, 2:24).

Both the male's and female's rectitude are identical in the larger sense. There are no special preferences for skin color, physical features, or mental capabilities that God allows to occur. But there are designed complementarities (relative differences) in strengths, weaknesses, emotional preferences, and utility between the sexes. These require close unity between male and female to accomplish their mission and procreate.

The thrust of identity politics today has attempted to blur many of these natural differences. But they do exist as intended by God, not to the point of exclusion, but rather of cooperation. In other words, we're designed to need each other.

Your Existence

God created you the moment you were conceived in your mother's womb. You got your body from your parents, and your soul from God. The gift of life in your soul caused your body to start growing, and the rest is history.

Before you, there was nothing. Should God withdraw his creative intent for you, even for an instant, you would cease to be, as though you had never existed.

Every blink of the eye, every breath you draw, every sin you commit, every act of compassion you accomplish, can happen only because God holds you in existence, moment to moment.

The good news is—God promised Noah after the flood that he would never again destroy mankind. Your existence depends both on God's creative will and his faithfulness. Count on it.

Submission

At the beginning, God put Adam and Eve in a perfect place called the Garden of Eden. They were created *beings* with free will, and had to choose whether or not to follow the rules, pursue their mission, and live in the garden. They disobeyed. Sin, death, and evil entered our world (more on that later).

We, too, must choose whether or not to live our lives obeying God's rules. But we cannot decide to obey God, once and for all, in a single moment. When sin and death entered, mankind became creatures of time and circumstance.

Your person develops over time. You acquire knowledge, encounter threats, opportunities, and make decisions, every day. You're not the same person as yesterday, and you'll be different tomorrow. So, your submission is measured, in part, by the state of your character and the cumulative decisions you execute from one moment to the next.

Judgment

At some point in your life, God will call you to judgment. Your natural life will end, and your soul will live for eternity. The status of your soul will be judged as to whether or not: 1) it is worthy of the Beatific Vision (entering Heaven), 2) it requires additional purification, or 3) you have chosen to reject God and live apart from him for eternity.

Almighty God is a God of love, mercy, and justice. The condition of your soul depends largely on the state of your character, as discussed above. None of us can predict with certainty the absolute condition of our souls. Only God is the perfect Judge.

1. If you are judged worthy of Heaven, you will enter into its wonders for eternity.

2. If you are judged to require additional purification, you will enter a 2.state of punishment (often called Purgatory) until you are ready to enter Heaven. But you will certainly get to Heaven eventually.

3. If at death you are unrepentant of debauchery, immorality, violence, and other grave evils, your soul is in serious jeopardy. If you are judged by God to have rejected his invitation to your intended destiny, you will be sentenced to eternal punishment.

The traditional explanation of this punishment is the fires of Hell.

> If your hand causes you to stumble, cut it off; it is better for
> you to enter life maimed than to have two hands and to go
> to hell, to the unquenchable fire (Mk 9:45).

Some people question if the burning fires of Hell are sufficient
punishment for the rejection of infinite love. Others contend that a
worse punishment is living for eternity—alone, dunked in evil, without
God, love, companionship, hope, or peace.

These are sobering words. They have often been used to scare people
into doing good and following God's laws. But in the long run, following
God out of fear is counterproductive and can easily fail. Thus, it's
important to keep before you the very clear choice placed there by God.

He has created you, given you a rectitude ordained by him, and a
mission with an intended destiny. You have free will and his guaranty
of support. But make no mistake. You will be judged, and failure brings
incredibly painful punishment for eternity.

Accessible God

That you exist proves that God loves you. That you continue to exist
proves it even more. No matter how difficult life can become, you can
trust that God is there, loving you, ready to help you make the right
choices.

He's a loving Father, watching out for you, making sure you retain free
will, and your struggles are a fair fight. He wants you to succeed in your
quest. He's accessible. He's got your back.

You're going to need help working through opportunities, failures, and
threats in life. You're going to need an independent source of wisdom
and discernment to sort things out—available only through your
ongoing personal relationship with God, from the Holy Spirit, whom
Jesus promised.

> When the Spirit of truth comes, he will guide you into all the
> truth... (Jn 16:13 RSV)

Evil and Redemption

So, you were created from nothing by a Triune God, intended to live with him in Heaven. Next, it's best to know your enemy. Working your way through life making choices, pursuing dreams, and choosing God is hard enough, but you'll have to deal with an enemy who wants you to fail.

Some people think stories about evil and *evil beings* are just an excuse for bad decisions and bad behavior. But the Bible and the catechism of the Catholic Church makes it clear:

> *...evil is not an abstraction, but refers to a person, Satan, the Evil One, the angel who opposes God. The devil (dia-bolos) is the one who "throws himself across" God's plan and his work of salvation accomplished in Christ (CCC 2851).*

Your enemy's name is Satan, or the devil. His followers are known as evil spirits, or demons. Satan and his followers hate you because you're able to enter Heaven and they've lost their chance. But their main objective is to wage war against God. Should you fail to choose God during life, evil will have defeated God's plan for another soul.

There are those trying to make life easier by denying evil. But hiding in denial will not be successful. You will be tempted in many ways, and perhaps have been already. It's imperative that you understand the enemy, their tactics, and how to effectively resist them.

Here are a few very important points.

- Satan and his spirits are not, and never were, equal or superior to God.
- Jesus, the Son of God, has totally defeated Satan and his spirits.
- Evil can tempt us, but can never overpower us beyond our free will.

Angels

Before Adam and Eve, God created a vast number of angels to be with him in Heaven. He gave them free will, and overwhelming beauty and power. But they could not move in with God until they chose freely to be there.

So, God gave them an opportunity to choose through an act of submission. Satan, the most beautiful and powerful angel of them all, decided to enter Heaven through his own power, instead of receiving it as a gift through obedience.

His choice is called the "sin of the angels," a sin of pride: *Refusing to submit to their rectitude defined by a superior [being].*

Satan seduced one-third of the heavenly host to join with him. A great battle followed in the heavens. Michael, the archangel, with the rest of the heavenly host, defeated Satan and his followers, casting them out of Heaven into the fires of Hell.

Original Sin

Adam and Eve's level of existence did not yet qualify them to enter

Heaven. God put them in a perfect place called the Garden of Eden. They had great food and lodging, perfect weather, and walked and talked with God. If mosquitoes existed then, they were probably harmless.

Like the angels, Adam and Eve had free will and were given a test so they could choose to stay in the garden. Satan tempted Eve, who then tempted Adam, to disobey God. They failed their test and were ejected from the garden.

Adam and Eve's sin is called "original sin"; it was a spiritual train wreck. The damage from their sin is passed on to all human beings, a sort of spiritual DNA from which there was no recovery.

- Our relationship with God was damaged. Some describe this condition as having a hole in us that can only be filled with God.
- They had sinned against an infinite Being. There was no way to repair such a breach.
- They were locked out of the Garden and Heaven forever.
- Evil gained entry into our world to harass you, tempt you, and deceive you away from God.
- Satan brought death with him, but not just physical death.
- Once an obedient servant to mankind in the Garden, nature is unruly, able to kill or starve you.
- Your will is easily overcome by emotion and desires.
- Your spiritual authority is weakened.

Evil's Tactics

Evil never stops trying to nudge you away from God's will and his love for you. Four tactics used most often are: Temptation, Accusation, Deception, and Overkill.

Temptation is the most frequent tactic, usually linked to an emotion, a desire, or an appetite. You encounter something that is not proper for you at the time; into your mind comes a thought you should take it or do it anyway.

Nothing is off-limits, anything can be attacked. The rationale that justifies yielding is always a lie, often with a grain of truth to make it believable: It's not that important, nobody will care, you won't get caught, I want it anyway, and so on.

Accusations are aggressive thoughts that you have done something seriously wrong, unforgiveable. You've created a mess from which you'll never get out. Whether or not you've actually done something wrong, guilt is heaped on you, driving you away from God's love and forgiveness into a sense of hopelessness.

Deception consists of lies, many lies, again with a grain of truth, woven together over a period time. They lead you to take action or make a decision you would otherwise not do.

Overkill is one of the cleverest. Evil gets alongside your righteous actions, urging you to do more and more, pressing beyond reason. Overkill can turn a good action that would bring life and blessing into discord, often cancelling the intended good or reversing the effect.

Thoughts can come from your mind, your emotions, from God, or from evil. Evil's attacks are defeated mostly through the will and by the truth. Jesus said: "...the truth will make you free" (Jn 8:32). Just getting a few facts, or asking a few questions, can quickly dissolve deception and emotional inertia.

If you decide a thought is from evil, just say no, and reject it from your mind. Just saying no is hard to do when an emotion or appetite is raging and demanding satisfaction. In a very difficult situation, rejecting the thought "in the name of Jesus" can be effective.

Your ability to control emotions, appetites, and desires through your will is a vital tool in life. Exercises to strengthen the will through occasional denial are very helpful and will be discussed later.

Redeemer Son

Out of love for us, the Father sent his Son to cancel the claims of death and pay the price of our freedom. By the power of the Holy Spirit, the Son was incarnated of the Virgin Mary (a theological term that best represents how the Son acquired mankind's rectitude).

The Son of God became man, taking on himself the plight of all mankind, past, present, and future. By his shed blood on the Cross, he purchased our freedom from the grip of evil and defeated Satan, once and for all.

Defeated by Jesus, evil spirits remain envious of us. They never stop trying to deprive us of our inheritance, using our pride, appetites, emotions, and desires against us.

So now life is getting complicated. Here are a few essential facts:

- The devil and evil spirits are real enemies.

   Be sober, be watchful. Your adversary the devil prowls around like a roaring lion, seeking someone to devour (1 Pet 5:8 RSVCE).

- Choosing to obey God requires you to handle two kinds of temptations that often work together: The train wreck of your Adamic nature (the effects of original sin), and temptations from evil spirits.
- Jesus will not allow us to be tempted beyond our ability to resist.
- We are guaranteed all the necessary wisdom and power to win the fight. Through Jesus' sacrifice, baptism, the other sacraments of the Church, and your own relationship with God, an unlimited supply of grace is at hand to protect, instruct, and equip you in your struggles.

The Bible

The Bible is a collation (arranged collection) of sacred writings (books) used by Christians for over twenty centuries now. It consists of two parts, the Old Testament, and the New Testament.

Several versions were in use during the early centuries AD (Anno Domini, Latin for "the year of our Lord."). In 1563 AD, the Church officially approved a complete text derived from old texts written in Hebrew, Latin and Greek. There are many modern translations of the approved text as scholars gain insights into the meaning of the older ones.

Next to the Eucharist, the Bible is the most important support for success in life. It's a record of God's revelation of himself to his people.

But God doesn't reveal himself in a first-person narrative. Instead, he is revealed through stories, tradition, and inspired revelation, handed down over the centuries. They record God's encounters with the ancient Hebrew people, the life of Jesus, and of the early Christians.

How God treats his Chosen People, with all their imperfections and sins, reveals countless insights into God's love for us and how to handle the challenges of life.

The Church teaches that the Bible is an inspired word of God; that the

Holy Spirit influenced the words, message, and collation. The Bible is incapable of error in matters of faith and morals, but not necessarily in historic or scientific matters.

> All scripture is inspired by God and profitable for teaching, for reproof, for correction, and for training in righteousness (2 Tim 3:16).

The Old Testament

The Old Testament is the largest part of the Bible and, with some exceptions, coincides with the Hebrew Bible. The Hebrew text includes stories, traditions, poetry, and history passed down from generation to generation as books.

Long thought to be inspired, efforts to collate the sacred books into a Hebrew Bible began around 500 BC. The Hebrew canon, a list of books that make up their Holy Scripture, was mostly complete by 200 BC.

Incorporation of the Hebrew Bible into the canon of the Christian Bible is a powerful statement about the roots of Christianity. Important theology, regulations, forms of worship, and religious practices in the Jewish faith have been modified or replaced in Christianity.

The extent of these changes might suggest that Christianity is a stand-alone religion, entirely separate from the Jewish faith. But that is incorrect. The appearance of Jesus as the Son of God, his sacrifice and promise of a new life, fulfilled God's long-standing promise to the Chosen People, and opened his special relationship with them to everyone.

Christianity completes the work God began with Abraham 4,000 biblical years ago. Mankind's relationship with God has been restored and we're able, at last, to get to Heaven. Our roots remain in the Chosen People. Indispensable wisdom and insight are recorded in the Hebrew Bible. Mining its contents will be richly rewarded.

The New Testament

The smaller section of the Bible records the beginning of Christianity with accounts of the life of Jesus, followed by letters from apostles and evangelists written to groups in the Christian community throughout the world.

First is a group of four books called Gospels, which means "good news." They are independent accounts of the life of Jesus. Three of the four books were written by a different apostle—Matthew, Mark, and John—with a unique, inspired emphasis. A fourth was written by Luke, a physician and disciple. They are not identical, and they contain a substantial amount of historical accuracy.

Following the Gospels is the fifth book, called Acts, which records various acts of the apostles, also written by the Luke. His book relates activities of the Church beginning with the Ascension, Pentecost, and the early period through 90 AD.

Next are a group of letters called Epistles, letters written to churches in various cities. The largest number were written by Saul of Tarsus (St. Paul), a Jew who persecuted members of the Church at first. He was blinded and knocked off his horse by an overpowering light on his way to more persecutions in Damascus. He converted after this miraculous event and became a vigorous evangelist and prolific writer.

The last book is the Apocalypse, or book of Revelation. It was written by the Apostle John about 90 AD, on the island of Patmos. It's a prophetic book describing a series of visions received by John, including messages to the various churches at the time.

The imagery appears to be literal in some places and symbolic in others. There are many different interpretations. Some believe the visions refer to the apostolic era, or the first century. Others believe the symbolic descriptions address the struggle between good and evil or the end times.

Bible Study

You can't get to know the Bible, often called the word of God, at one sitting or in a month, or a year. It takes a lifelong commitment of prayerful study to plumb its depths and reveal its wisdom. People have read the Bible for years and years, only to find a passage that appears totally new.

As you begin your study, ask the Holy Spirit to guide and enlighten you to understand the Scriptures and their meaning. Many people comment that the Holy Spirit helps them see and understand things they never saw before. That may not happen every time, but it does happen a lot.

At first, commit to daily Bible study for a limited time, say 5 minutes, or 15. Don't try too much. Pay attention to the story and history as it develops. During your reading, ask questions of yourself: What is God doing here? What are these people doing here? Is there a message here for me?

You may or may not receive inspiration at first, but eventually it will happen as you become more familiar with the content and learn how to listen, what to look for. Thank the Holy Spirit after each session.

It's best to begin in the book of Genesis and read the first few chapters. Then switch to one of the Gospels and the Acts to get an overall picture. It's not important to read the Bible sequentially, all the way through. But it is important to read all of it. It's okay to skip boring or troublesome passages for a while and skip backwards and forwards as the Holy Spirit leads.

There are helpful study guides that explain the organization and content of the books in more detail. There are also charts and graphs that show calendar timelines for the period each book is addressing.

A growing, long-term acquaintance between you, the Bible, and the Holy Spirit will serve you well for a lifetime.

Religion

Religions are organizations around a body of facts, beliefs, and support systems held in common by their believers. Their interests are typically about the purpose of life and creation, pursuing a relationship with God or gods, and supporting the believers in their pursuits.

There are four major religions in the world: Christianity, Islam, Hinduism, and Buddhism (Britannica). They each recognize one God in loosely similar ways, but vary significantly about other major beliefs. We will focus on Christianity and the Catholic Church, as in the earlier presentations.

Jesus

The Jews had long anticipated the arrival of a Messiah, or Savior, who would deliver them from the many persecutions and sufferings they experienced as the Chosen People. In the year 3 BC, about 1,500 years after Moses, a Jew named Jesus was born in Bethlehem, Judea, and grew up in Galilee.

He was raised in the Jewish faith and practiced his religion faithfully. At the age of 30, he began a teaching/preaching ministry. It didn't contradict the Jewish religion, but expanded on it, and introduced some new concepts. Among these were: God is a God of love, we should forgive our enemies (turn the other cheek), and forsake revenge and retribution.

He attracted a large following because he performed many physical miracles, cast out evil spirits, and raised two people from the dead. Then, towards the end, he said he was the Son of God, that mankind must be born again, and we must eat his flesh and drink his blood to sustain this new life.

Finally, he said he would rise from the dead three days after his death, and told his disciples he would send the Holy Spirit to be with them and us forever. All of these claims were outrageous heresy to the Jewish leaders, and they delivered him to the Romans to be crucified.

Jesus was crucified in 30 AD and did rise from his tomb three days later. He appeared to many of his followers, as recorded in Scriptures. After 40 days, he ascended into Heaven in the presence of his disciples. Ten days later, the Holy Spirit descended on the disciples at Pentecost, which marks the birthday of Christianity.

Other religions of the world have a significant body of claims, theology, and practices. But the joyous cries that Jesus' disciples must have shouted on Easter Monday emanated from an event unmatched in eternity: "He's alive!" "He's alive!" "He's Alive!"

Catholic Christianity

The small group of disciples expanded rapidly as they spread out announcing this man, Jesus, who had died on a cross to redeem us from original sin, rose from the dead, and offers a new life through baptism. They became known as Christians after the Greek word *Christos*, which means "the anointed one."

Soon, Christianity was headquartered in Rome and known as the Catholic (meaning universal) Church throughout the world. A small branch that developed from the early evangelists is located in Eastern Europe.

The Roman church was headed by the pope, and continues uninterrupted as the Catholic Church. The smaller Eastern church still retains and practices all of the Christian teachings and traditions traceable back to the apostles. It's known as the Orthodox Church.

In 1517 AD, a German priest and professor of theology named Martin Luther announced a list of 95 complaints about Church practices and theology. He refused to renounce them and was excommunicated (expelled from the Church). This began what is known as the Protestant Reformation.

Over the years following, a growing number of groups split off from the Catholic Church or started their own churches, claiming to be following Jesus as Christians. Today there are ten or so separate Protestant and Evangelical Churches. Their beliefs and practices vary from the Catholic Church in several significant ways.

Catholic Church

The Roman Catholic Church claims to be the one, true, apostolic church— directly descended from the apostles. The Eastern church is apostolic but doesn't recognize the authority of the pope. Their sacraments and teachings are recognized by the Roman church as valid.

All of the Christian churches base their beliefs in part on the Bible. Teachings of the Protestant and Evangelical Churches go back only to the day they started. Further back, they rely on Catholic teachings, to the extent they accept them.

The Catholic Church recognizes the Protestant and Evangelical Churches as separated brethren, and together with all believers is formed the Body of Christ.

Roman Catholic teachings and traditions include three important features that are not fully endorsed by the other Churches. The *Teaching Magisterium* is guided by the Holy Spirit as the Church defines an unbroken, growing body of practices and revealed truths of the faith. They were handed down from the preaching of Jesus and teachings of the apostles.

27

The magisterium also provides advice and rules to assist your efforts to get close to God. These involve worship, administration of the sacraments, and validation of new teachings and insights into the faith.

The *papal office* is directly descended from Apostle Peter, who was appointed head of the Church by Jesus himself. Together with the bishops, the pope is authorized to rule the Church as the representative of Christ. Only in serious issues of faith and morals are the pope's pronouncements infallible, and he must declare it so.

There are *seven sacraments* in the Catholic Church. They each confer special graces; powers that come forth from the Body of Christ.

1. Baptism—You receive the new life promised by Jesus to replace your Adamic life inherited at conception.

2. Confirmation—Your grasp of the Holy Spirit that you received at baptism is strengthened and the Spirit is more fully released to prepare you for life's struggles.

3. Eucharist—This is *the centerpiece* of the Catholic Church, a reenactment of Jesus' death and resurrection called the sacrifice of the Mass. During the consecration, the priest says specific words from the Last Supper. The bread and wine are actually transformed into the body and blood of Christ, while retaining their original form.

    The faithful receive this consecrated bread and wine in holy communion, just as the apostles did at the Last Supper when Jesus consecrated bread and wine saying: "...this is my body," and "...this is my blood..." (Mt 26:26,28 NRSV).

    The Eucharistic miracle is called *the real presence*. It can only be performed by an ordained Catholic priest and is one of the primary differences between the Catholic and other Christian Churches.

Through him, with him, and in him... Amen!

4. Penance—Sometimes called confession, an ordained priest, as a representative of Christ, forgives your sins, restores your relationship with God, offers advice, and assigns acts of penance to strengthen your will.

5. Anointing of the Sick—Done with a special oil, the sacrament is administered for those suffering illness, or otherwise needing healing. Along with penance and Viaticum (Holy Communion), the sacrament provides graces to prepare for the end-of-life journey and face death.

6. Holy Orders—Specially trained men, called by God to serve the Church, are ordained with graces and powers to dispense

the sacraments, preach, and support the faithful. It's a lifetime commitment.

7. Matrimony—Confers special graces that help the married couple form a union, develop a family that's open to children, and provide strength to survive the rigors of married life.

Office of the Faithful

The preceding information about the magisterium, the papacy, and the sacraments, describes priests, bishops, and other official church offices that carry significant, ordained responsibilities. Their positions garner considerable reverence and esteem.

However, it's a deception to so elevate the importance of the ordained that your own importance is minimized. The deception intends to shackle the execution of your own responsibilities. The Church teaches that by baptism, you are incorporated into Christ and *fully* share in the priestly, prophetic, and kingly office of Christ (CCC 897).

You have significant responsibilities in the kingly office, worthy of reverence and esteem as well—evangelization, marriage, commerce, governance, and yes, even prophecy and prayers for healing. Jesus sent all of his disciples forth, not just the apostles.

> The seventy returned with joy, saying, "Lord, in your name even the demons submit to us!" He said to them, "I watched Satan fall from heaven like a flash of lightning. See, I have given you authority to tread on snakes and scorpions, and over all the power of the enemy; and nothing *will* hurt you. Nevertheless, do not rejoice at this, that the spirits submit to you, but rejoice that your names are written in heaven" (Lk 10:17–20 NRSVCE).

The Church manages the Church. You have a significant task in the office of Christ as well—manage the world. Is there overlap? Yes; but never minimize or impoverish the faithful's role.

Discernment

God's righteousness is activated in your life by discarding old, Adamic weaknesses, thus releasing Jesus' new life. You develop life-giving habits and reject death-dealing ones. Your character is re-formed by love, goodness, purity, obedience, integrity, moral rectitude, and other virtues.

Discernment is called for when integrity confronts a choice between bad and good, or even amongst variations of good.

Integrity

A single, core group of values you embrace is called your *worldview*. It's the *reason why* for your actions, beliefs, methods, measures, and principles. As water feeds the tree from its roots by osmosis, people acquire values and priorities as they interact in relationships and society at large.

You must make a deliberate effort in your travels to be conscious of what values are in play, determine if they're consistent with God's values, and decide which ones to adopt or reject. If you haven't yet decided about your worldview, someone else is doing it for you by cultural osmosis.

Your worldview need not be rigid, an iron-clad system refusing to consider change. Change should be possible, but seldom; adjusted only when harmony is maintained and the core remains consistent with God's values.

Integrity means your actions are consistent with your worldview at all times, and includes a sense of wholeness, honesty, and authenticity. You have achieved integrity when actions driven by your major values are correctly anticipated by others.

Achieving integrity is a lifetime effort, just like developing your character. You must faithfully execute a commitment to make decisions independent of outside influences and your own weaknesses. Reputations are gained through experience, not promises.

But note well that actions, faithful to a set of values, do not necessarily predict a good outcome. It's all about the values, so choose wisely. *Both Hitler and Jesus Christ had solid integrity. Their actions each were consistent with their values. But the results were miles apart.*

Regular Discernment

Natural discernment. You're born able to diagnose situations, then choose amongst them. It's a primary tool that makes us human, apart from the rest of creation.

Unfortunately, your natural gift is uninformed and untrained at the beginning. You're easily misled by fervid desires and the deceptions of evil. At best, natural discernment matures in just one or a few areas.

Worldly wisdom. Discernment matures in the training, education, and experience we receive in life. But many of us don't get proper education, training, mentoring, and formation of our natural discernment capabilities as we grow up. So, we have to learn from our mistakes.

How fast your worldly wisdom grows depends on your willingness to change your behavior, and your ability to effectively manage your emotions and appetites.

Spiritual wisdom. Your spiritual abilities need formation, just like your natural abilities. You received the *new life* of Jesus and the Holy Spirit at baptism. The Scriptures tell us we must die to our Adamic self in order to fully release, and be transformed into, this *new life*.

> Put to death therefore what is earthly in you ...put off the old nature with its practices and... put on the new nature, which is being renewed in knowledge after the image of its creator. (Col 3:5, 9–10 RSV).

The death/new life process involves crucial choices. The Holy Spirit is your advocate to help you make the right ones. He warns you, affirms you, and points you in the right direction.

God doesn't talk all the time, but more often than you think. He speaks to each of us differently. Mistakes are possible. Evil, your intellect, appetites, and the culture of the world suggest things all the time.

It takes time and testing to recognize God's voice. You have to ask, listen, then test the thoughts you receive. Those from God will be consistent with Scripture, church teaching, and can also be confirmed by a mature Christian. Be assured, you can learn to recognize God's voice and grow in confidence that he is with you, side by side, 24/7.

Discernment of Spirits

The Gift of the Discernment of Spirits. There's an old saying that evil can appear to us as angels of light. Evil doesn't care if you do a *good* thing or a *bad* thing, just not the *God* thing.

Evil uses threats of guilt or fear, the demands of exaggerated emotional appetites, and deceptive temptations. The deceptions and accusations often happen when you're tired, stressed-out, under pressure, lonely, even hungry. The spirits know our buttons and how to push them.

The discernment of spirits is a gift of the Holy Spirit. He's your coach, helping you see through outer wrappings and expose the true nature of temptation and deception. With that truth you are certain to deny them influence in your actions.

There are five fairly common ways in which the discernment of spirits is encountered.

1. You are thinking about or have begun travelling a road toward an objective. But an overall sense of *grayness* or *brooding*, a significant foreboding, occurs in your spirit. "I don't think this is going anywhere." Do not proceed toward your objective. Check things out with a mature Christian before continuing.

2. An action you're considering seems OK. The motive is sound, it's scripturally consistent, within your resources, and you have a genuine desire to accomplish it.

   But somehow, it just doesn't seem quite right. You have no "release" to begin. "It just doesn't seem right yet." This is what many people call *a check in my spirit.* It's best to wait, don't force. Wait until things are clear and you sense a release to begin.

3. You're in a righteous situation, but *spiritual life starts draining* from you. Doubts begin to creep in and your motive seems weaker. Your confidence, sense of joy in the Lord, and certainty of your actions seems to drain away. "This is really getting hard. Is this really what God wanted me to do?"

   Still, you remain convinced of the righteousness of your efforts. If you didn't force your way past a check in your spirit, you can dismiss whatever is draining your spirit and continue on. The Holy Spirit convicts and brings life; he does not accuse or bring doubt.

4. You get a clear sense that a spirit, or an evil tactic is at work. "I think a spirit of anxiety is attacking me!" This may or may not be a *direct revelation*. It is unreliable because it's perceived through your own bias, agenda, and experience. Specific

confirmation with Scripture and a mature Christian is required before action.

5. An easy, or perhaps even difficult, road lies ahead. Emotional demands, agendas, and strategies for fame and fortune are absent. There is a *quiet, confident yes* about it; "This thing must be done by me." Be assured, the Lord is with you, and you are acting in his plan.

All these types of discernment work together in real time. You receive guidance from the Holy Spirit through your relationship with God; a relationship that grows and matures, helping you recognize his voice.

It's always time to approach God. He loves you; always waiting to get close. So, talk to God, listen for him, learn about him, spend time with him, get to know him. He's available, and he's waiting.

Emotions, Sex and the Mind

Emotions

You are a unique creature because you can think and act independently. Your *intellect* allows you to know, assess, analyze, draw conclusions, and make decisions. Your *will* executes those decisions.

Emotions are tools to support your activities, not run them. They provide situational awareness through feelings. They can be very helpful, but not always. Fear that shrieks in situations of significant danger helps your intellect decide—run quickly! But an unreasonable fear of failure will stifle productivity and growth.

Left to themselves, emotions can take off and escalate into exhaustion. They are a powerful influence, but impulsive—running hot one day, and rejecting yesterday's hottie the next. They involve themselves in everything, invited or not.

Emotions don't discriminate amongst priorities in your life. Instead, they are tied to your various attachments. A loss by your favorite team can be just as emotional as losing your wallet. So, when it comes to your decision processes, the intellect has to first separate emotional wheat from the chaff.

Powerful emotions, aligned with deep attachments or desires, are a force to be reckoned with. They're a challenge begging to be managed, and that's a job for the will.

Adam and Eve's authority was severely weakened because of their sin. A major effect was weakening the will; they passed it on to you. That's why it's hard work to make the emotions obey.

There are two ways emotions can be tamed. Self-control through *denial* has been successfully practiced in Christianity for centuries. Desires and appetites are deliberately denied for short periods, such as not eating certain foods, or avoiding TV—whatever needs to be taken down a peg or two.

Emotions respond demanding satisfaction. You ignore the demand and continue what you're doing or switch to something else. The struggle is significant the first few times you do this, especially if a habit has been formed. But each time it gets easier as your will gains more control.

The second tactic is to *reduce the degree of attachment*. Revise the priorities you assign to certain attachments. If you don't like rutabagas, its absence from a menu won't gather much emotion.

There is still another way attachments can be reduced; through your relationship with God. Alone, without God, mankind seeks peace, satisfaction, a sense of worth, mission, and so on, through worldly pursuits.

As your relationship with God deepens, attachments to worldly things will decrease and lose significance. They can still provide an abundant measure of comfort, pleasure, and satisfaction. But coming closer to God will increase your trust in our Lord's love and provision for you.

You'll learn to wait on the Lord and discern amongst your wants, needs, and his leadings. Your emotions will have much less to be concerned about, and the only losses will be anxiety, striving, and a sense of being alone.

Sex Overview

This section is an overview about sex to plant a foundation for more details discussed in the chapters on dating and marriage.

Maturity is measured by how well key features of humanity are integrated in the individual: emotions, accountability, integrity, sexuality, love, God's values, and other characteristics. If one or another of these features is running out of balance, wild, or not at all, it must be brought into balance and order. It takes time and hard work to move through the integration process. Significant character and value changes happen frequently.

Mankind's mission from God consists of two parts; manage the world, and procreate. The sex drive is not an emotion, although emotions get involved. It's not a desire, either, although desire often occurs. Sex is a category all by itself. It's a powerful need in us that strives to be used; right up there with survival.

Sex is intended for marriage. Its full promise is released in the lifelong gift of a fully integrated man and woman in a marriage partnership. It's planted in you by Almighty God with a dual purpose: create people intended to live with him, and bless one another in the marriage relationship.

You are required to withhold sexual activity until marriage. Because you are a composite being of spirit and body, a struggle already exists in you between *spirit* and *flesh*. It's your heritage from original sin (CCC 2516).

Denying sexual activity is a very difficult task, especially with your weakened will and a society that rejects any restraints. A great source of guidance is the catechism of the Catholic Church.

There are two key virtues that assist and protect your efforts at restraint: chastity, and purity of heart. Each of these requires its own commitment and investment.

Chastity means a successful integration of sexuality and its passions in your character, made possible by the Holy Spirit through baptism.

Chastity is apprenticeship in self-mastery, a training in human freedom. Dignity is achieved by ridding himself of all slavery to the passions, and, by his diligence and skill, effectively integrating his sexuality (CCC 2339, freely edited).

A marriage candidate's appeal depends, to a large degree, on how well the elements of his humanity are integrated. Are they all present, in balance, and under control? Is there one or more hiding below the surface that still needs work? In other words: Is what you see, what you'll get?

If his sexuality has been running free, it's quite likely he'll be a different person after he's integrated. If he hasn't integrated his emotions, accountability, integrity, sexuality, love, God's values, and other characteristics, he's a problem already.

Purity of heart refers to how much your intellect and will is faithful to the way in which God requires you to live out your rectitude. There are four primary behaviors: Charity—the practice of agápe love; Chastity—successful sexual integration; Love of truth—in words and deeds; Orthodoxy of faith—values and practices consistent with the faith.

Purity of heart can be summed up in these key signatures:

- Seeking education in the moral law
- Disciplining your feelings and imagination, refusing impure thoughts
- Communicating with God regularly in prayer
- Protecting the dignity of others with modesty in speech, the eyes, dress, and words
- Avoiding lies, dissembling, gossip, and character assassination
- Maintaining mental purity by avoiding exposure to eroticism, voyeurism, and illusion

Sex is a highly restricted blessing. Nevertheless, it emphasizes the special importance of procreation in the heart of an infinitely loving God. Hard work is clearly in store. But take comfort and courage in the graces, wisdom, and good counsel available through the sacraments, the Church, and your relationship with God.

Managing the Mind

The organ inside your head and the intellect received from your soul is interchangeably and collectively referred to as your mind. It's one of the most overlooked in your tool set to receive training and development.

Training the mind's ability to focus, memorize, and acquire information begins early in life, typically in school. Later, the skills to analyze are expanded in higher education. But most of us know that when school is out, the mind defaults to free thinking.

Science has revealed a lot about how the physiology of the brain works. But little information exists about how to analyze, discriminate amongst input, compose alternatives, and recognize the difference between evil's input or input from God. Yet we are called to perform these actions countless times a day.

The mind can be controlled by force of will to focus on a specific objective for a long time. A musician must learn how to produce the notes with his instrument, understand the score and its meaning, and master the ability to render that meaning in a performance. His probability of success depends on the effort he has invested and his creative talent.

Most of us get along pretty well with our limited skill in managing such a powerful instrument as the mind. But in my experience, people with a high level of creativity have great difficulty. The intellect floods their mind with possibilities, ideas, and random thoughts that can almost overwhelm.

It's a joy for the creative person to experience such a cornucopia of thoughts and awareness. But left unmanaged, creativity can be quite demanding, and interfere with pressing activities and needs. The creative person's mental activity is so far beyond normal they are easily bored and get frustrated with no place to express themselves.

Training a powerful instrument like the mind is analogous to breaking a horse. Horses are large, powerful animals. They can run fast, like a thoroughbred, pull huge weight, like a Clydesdale, or be sure-footed on the mountain trail.

But none of this happens until the horse is *broken;* the hard way, as in the Wild West, or the modern, cushy way, in a swimming pool. He must be trained to accept a human rider, a bit in his mouth, reins for steering, and training for his intended service. Absent this process, the powerful animal can accomplish little but run around in the wild seeking food and shelter.

In a similar way, the mind will run wild until it's *broken;* not abused or damaged, but submissive to your will as God intended. The task is far more difficult than with the emotions. Attempt to pray fifteen minutes straight without drifting, and you'll experience a mind that prefers to romp in the wild.

No matter how disciplined, a creative mind will always be looking in many directions and thinking a lot of thoughts. But it can be disciplined to focus in certain areas without distractions, at least for a limited time.

Just as in controlling emotions, a deliberate program of denial helps to give your will the upper hand. Then, when the creative juices are flowing freely, you can confidently say, "Stop, concentrate on this."

A creative mind is a blessing to its recipient and a gift to us all. The gift needs to pursue its capabilities and created potential. Control by the will is necessary to assist the revelation of its promise.

Love and Dating

About Love

Your rectitude allows you to know and to love. You can know and enjoy God in his glory at a level second only to the angels in Heaven. You can experience God's love for you and your love for others—a wonder, happiness, and peace that animals, rocks, and trees cannot know.

Like God, love is the centerpiece of your existence. The Scriptures use three Greek words for love, all part of the broader concept: *eros*, *filios*, and *agápe*.

Eros and *erotic* are words used mostly about sexual matters today. But eros means much more. It's a righteous aspect of love. It signals a preference or desire through the emotions. *I just love chocolate...that golf club...that hot car...that movie...etc.*

Eros' responses help you make selections. But eros only reveals surface preferences. Like emotions, eros is fickle—hot one minute and cold the next. This volatility makes you an easy target for evil, tempting you into excesses.

God created sexual desire in you to enliven a marriage commitment and foster procreation. It can easily mingle with eros, as in adolescent boy/girl falling in love, and infatuation with famous personalities. The initial attraction is eros, a simple preference. But when sexual desire attaches, emotional involvement increases substantially, and care must be taken to keep things in control.

Eros is an uncomplicated attraction to a person, situation, or things. It's an important tool in selecting candidates for initial dating or friendship. But like anything else, excesses or lack of control in eros can lead you into dark places. Serious difficulties with sin, alcohol, recreational drugs, hard drugs, or even rock music groupies, all start with an erotic attraction.

Filios is brotherly love or deep friendship. It binds people together, often for a very long time. It's a virtuous love, free of sexual overtones, attraction, or involvement. Feelings of loyalty among friends, camaraderie among teammates, and sacrifice for one another are common traits of filios love.

Filios relationships can occur amongst men, women, or both. The hookup mentality and free sex in society today have almost destroyed the understanding of a righteous filios relationship. But successful relationships still occur amongst men and women, in deep commitment to one another, that are void of sexual content. It's filios love that makes this possible.

Agápe is God's love. It's far more robust than the emotional attachment of eros or the deep friendship of filios. Agápe is a self-sacrificing love that puts the needs of the beloved first, before self.

Agápe seeks expression. It cannot stand by and wait, it must act, and act in favor of the beloved. It's a love that brings life and growth to all in its care through genuine service to their needs.

Jesus told the disciples that they must serve others; not consider themselves above, but rather below (Matt 20:25–28). He invokes a slave's mentality, where every concern is first directed toward the life, needs, and happiness of the master.

So, how do you prevent being run over like a doormat? The answer is to serve *needs*, not *wants*. Needs involve the survival, protection, and development of the beloved. Without them, both life and growth suffer. *Wants* are emotionally based and impulsive; robust urges one moment and gone the next.

Practicing agápe and walking the line between needs and wants is difficult in a relationship. Priorities and the situation can change quickly. The key to success is communication. Regular, detailed discussions are vital to staying current in the pace of things and detecting the true needs of your agápe beloved.

Commandments and Dating

I was a teenager in the 1950s, and a parent of teenagers in the 1960s. The dating scene today has changed so much it's hardly recognizable to me. Some semblance of past norms remains in early teen culture, but past fifteen, it's a whole new thing.

The biggest change is about sex. In my day, sex was supposed to wait until marriage. Today, with improved condoms and the pill, people indulge in sex sometimes on the first date. Emotional pressure and stress in the dating scene is substantially higher than the "old days," especially for girls.

The emphasis on freewheeling sex in society has produced predictable results. Marriage failures are over 50%; unmarried births per year have risen 41% over the last fifty years—72% for blacks, and 54% for Hispanics (U.S. Census).

Following is my best effort to bring forward from earlier days those principles I believe are correct, regardless of their current popularity. So, let's start with what God has to say.

Here are the two famous commandments:

#6 Thou shalt not commit adultery (Ex 20:14 KJV). *Adultery* means having sex with someone outside of your own marriage, or from another marriage. The commandment also prohibits fornication (i.e., sex between unmarried people).

Fornication is about virginity. "I'm saving myself for my wife" (or husband). Every unmarried individual is a candidate for marriage. Sex with that candidate breaches their future marital pledge of fidelity before it can be made. A pristine gift of sexual fidelity, to be pledged in the marriage vow, is damaged on arrival.

The reverse is also true. Fornicating violates your own yet-to-be marriage commitment; certainly not a strong recommendation to prospective candidates.

Fornication and adultery are mortal sins. Here's the definition:

> Mortal sin destroys charity in the heart of man by a grave violation of God's law; it turns man away from God, who is his ultimate end and his beatitude, by preferring an inferior good to him (CCC 1855).

There is no wiggle room here. Adultery and fornication are grave disruptions in your relationship with God—no matter what everyone else is doing.

#9 Thou shalt not covet... thy neighbor's wife... (Ex 20:17). The emphasis here is on purity of heart. *Covet* means to crave, envy, or lust after something; an intense form of desire. It could be proper, as in: "I covet your prayers for my cancer to be healed."

But if the intensity is directed beyond the limits of a pure heart—chastity and modesty—it's a grave sin. Jesus said, "But I say to you that every one who looks at a woman lustfully has already committed adultery with her in his heart" (Mt 5:28 RSVCE).

In the old days, dating was about friendship and preparation for marriage. There was a four-step process that roughly followed the age progression of teenagers. It began with casual **group encounters** at parties, movies, etc. Paring and late-night activity was avoided.

The next level was called **dating**. Boys and girls would go out together as a couple, perhaps with other couples, to a movie, a dance, or some other public activity. The couple explored each other's personalities, character, likes, and dislikes. The process was considered experimental, and without burden. A single or several dates did not imply there would be others.

The third step was **going steady**. Dating continued, but only with the same person. The relationship deepened, exploring each other in more detail to assess the possibility of a marriage candidate. Revelations of integration, character, or values often caused a breakup, and the couple returned to individual dating.

The final step was **engagement**. Selection of the marriage partner was now complete. Commitment to each other was just short of the wedding vow. Important plans for married life were made: where to live, was there enough money to live on, how many children, work situations, and preparations for the marriage ceremony.

Sex was inappropriate and aggressively discouraged by parents, schools, and the culture in all four stages. Still, the process was alive. Falling in and out of adolescent love occurred as physical and emotional attachments played out. But there was plenty of opportunity for friendship, fun, and filios and agápe love.

Some pregnancies outside of marriage occurred, but far less than today. Marriages were much more stable. Out-of-wedlock births, even without the pill, were significantly lower. Everyone had enough quality time to pick the right mate.

Special Note to the Guys

God says you must set sex aside until marriage. In keeping with that, you're obligated to treat women respectfully and refrain from trying to manipulate them into sexual activity during the dating process. Becoming a man of God is essential for your success.

If you sire a child, you're responsible for that child's care and development up through age 18, at least. To shirk that responsibility is a significant damage to your character, a grave injustice to the child, to others who provide the care, and society at large. In the annals of manhood, it doesn't get any lower.

Special Note to the Gals

You are the last line of defense for righteous actions in the dating process. Thankfully, your power to say no, and have it stick, has been significantly fortified and endorsed by society today.

But, the age-old quip still holds true: "In adultery and fornication, the man wants sex and the woman wants love. Which one gets what they want?"

You will be strongly tested when it comes to losing a promising relationship by saying no. Being a woman of God is essential to helping you trust God for your future, especially when you're tempted to settle for the present.

For Both

Remember that nobody is perfect. Mistakes are made. God offers us opportunities through the Church to receive forgiveness and reconciliation for our mistakes. But don't forget—reconciliation may square things with God, but responsibility in this life for the results of your actions remains.

Marriage

Over and over, the question, "What's the secret of a successful marriage?" is asked by people from all walks of life. They're aware of the high divorce rate, and they want to beat the statistics. Following are some insights distilled from a successful marriage of 62 years.

Don't Get Divorced

Marriage is usually a "wild ride." When times get tough, feelings and egos get hurt and we stake out our territories. The ultimate solution always jumps to the front—*divorce*. We're tempted to throw in the towel, abandon efforts to forgive, adjust, and craft new growth in the relationship.

Evil attacks marriages constantly, trying to thwart God's plans for mankind. God's instructions for our *being* (rectitude) are: *"Be fruitful and multiply and fill the earth and subdue it" (Gen 1:28).* Two important capabilities to support these endeavors were installed in mankind during Eve's creation. They are: sex and marriage.

Marriage is a long-term proposition. It's not something that you try on like a pair of shoes. If you aren't committed to ride out the tough times, you'll wind up in divorce, adultery, or fornication. This prediction is well-documented in fact.

My wife and I married at the ages of 19 and 17; she was the youngest. We both came from broken families and were determined to see things through, whatever the cost. They said we were too young; no chance at success. Still, we vowed to each other that divorce would never be an option, would never be discussed; the word would never be used.

That is not the full secret of our 62-year marriage, but it kept us together long enough for God to work things out. We were tested frequently as character developed, preferences and priorities changed, and the vicissitudes of life intruded. But we stuck it out, learned to forgive and change, and threw ourselves into God's love for us, accepting his protection, wisdom, and encouragement.

Marriage is permanent. There are understandable cases of separation, even secular divorce, due to abuse or intransigence. But the marriage vows are permanent unless dissolved by the Church in an annulment.

If you don't start with an iron-clad, total, no-holding-back, nothing-up-either-sleeve commitment before God that your marriage is permanent—statistics already show the results are not promising. My half-joking advice to newlyweds is: "It gets better after 25 years."

Marital Mission

The marriage mission has five components.

1. **Marriage is a call from God to a ministry**. It's a sacrament; an *"...efficacious sign of grace, instituted by Christ and entrusted to the Church, by which divine life is dispensed to us"* *(CCC 1131)*.

2. Partner with God to create new life—people who receive their existence and an opportunity to live with God in Heaven.

3. Develop a stable relationship in which the husband and wife can

mature and grow in their relationship with God and each other.

4.   Foster a loving environment wherein children will be nurtured, matured, and mentored in their development.

5.   Provide building blocks for society—models for relationships on which larger elements of society can be formed; proof that relationships backed by God's love bring life and peace.

In marriage, the couple and God make a pact together—just the three of them (CCC 1623). They commit to participate in God's plans for mankind. He pledges to back it up with grace, love, and protection.

The priest "witnesses" the commitment, but he does not dispense the sacrament. It's God and the couple alone who confer the sacrament, and his personal involvement with the partnership is guaranteed forever.

When you think about it this way, the mission is awesome, almost overpowering. But we take comfort in the fact that God *"…makes present the graces proper to each sacrament. They bear fruit in those who receive them with the required dispositions" (CCC 1131)*. In other words, he's got your back.

If your relationship with God is the number one priority, a razor-thin close second is your marriage commitment. It ranks way above career, sex, money, power, and a host of other priorities in this hedonistic society.

Marital Threats

The glue that makes a marriage work is agápe love—a foundation of self-sacrificing, "godly love" that *puts the needs of the beloved first*. Married life is filled with opportunities to put your priorities at the service of your beloved and grow in character through the graces of agápe.

It takes time, a lot of effort, and pain to be skilled in agápe love—to freely forgive, be open to and respect the other's needs, acquire a willingness to change, and maintain a focus away from self.

Considering the significance of God's plan for marriage, it's no surprise the institution is under attack on all fronts. Our society is overrun with activities that weaken the concepts of commitment, sacrifice, deference to others, loyalty, and a host of other tools for marital success.

A major threat to marriage is fornication. It's unfortunate that many people engage in sex before marriage, turning God's righteous plan for sex upside down. They elevate sex higher than the sacrament, and their view of the marriage commitment is cheapened.

The full wonder of sex after marriage becomes adulterated. The risk of divorce is higher as character traits, previously masked by lust, are finally revealed. These effects are not always permanent, but it takes serious time and effort to make the proper adjustments.

Marital Tactics

Marriage is hard work and requires frequent attention. Each party must keep three balls in the air: their own relationship with God, the other party's needs, and the children. The needs often conflict, as do the relevant priorities.

Parenting adds its own responsibilities and blessings into the mix. Children are a source of unique joy and delight. Their talents and capabilities will amaze and bless you as you mentor their growth and skills.

Nevertheless, stressful challenges, opportunities for your character to grow, happen from time to time. In those times, it's helpful to remember you are caring for a person that Almighty God himself chose to exist. He has their back, as well as yours.

Character issues complicate priority selections even further. Each member of the family occupies a special place on the playing field of life. Their issues can vary significantly among them. When relationships get out of order, extra work is required to communicate, achieve forgiveness, and implement changes.

But none of us is properly trained to do this. We're all incompetent. Our culture prods us to focus on self, power, money, and emotional satisfaction. So, you must work extra hard to keep your marriage in play as you slog through life.

Every time you sense life being drained from the marriage, you must communicate, identify the issue(s), work hard to implement adjustments, and release the flow of agápe love. It's necessary work, and important work—the very foundation of the kingdom of God. He's on your side, and will provide the necessary grace.

There are wonderful benefits, pleasures, and joys in marriage that cannot be experienced any other way. You will be drawn closer to our Lord. Your character will mature, and the deepening relationship with your partner will be a constant source of love, peace, and fulfillment.

It's never easy. Just keep in mind that on the other side of forgiveness and sacrifice is new life and all of its blessings.

A Man of God

There are three principal characteristics that mark the man of God: 1) An ongoing relationship with God, 2) submission to Jesus as Lord of your life, and 3) a servant mentality. This chapter is not just about males, it's about men and women living their rectitude, their righteousness, their created intent as defined by God at conception.

> Be fruitful and multiply, and fill the earth and subdue it... (Gen 1:28).

God created man to govern the world and multiply, filling the earth in the process. But he quickly realized man needed a friend, a companion, someone to be with and share the load.

It couldn't be just another man like Adam. His partner needed equal footing to avoid any problems with hierarchy. But they had to need each other so they would stay working together.

God created Eve from Adam's being to share the same rectitude, but significant deficiencies and distinctions were planted in both. We assume Adam's appearance changed some from his original, but Eve's appearance and physiology was significantly different.

There is no legitimate justification for a man or woman to elevate the importance of their capabilities at the expense of the other; no justification to claim one sex is superior to the other. You are wired to need the other sex. Attempts to cleave these dependencies, and advance your personal importance, are cancers in our collective relationships.

You must celebrate the differences between men and women and the need/capability tension amongst us. You may treasure your contributions to success in life, but you must gratefully acknowledge the equally important, if significantly different, contributions of the opposite sex.

Close to God

Being a man of God means being someone who is faithfully living out his rectitude installed by God at conception. And it means carrying out that mission while being faithful to the instructions and values defined by your Creator.

Baptism freed you from the stain of Adam and Eve's sin. You received the new life promised by Jesus, and the way to Heaven is open. Now you must start a close relationship with God, a lifetime commitment, in order to make the most of this new life.

Your decision to start such a relationship is rooted in faith about who and what God is, and recognition of his love for you. Just like cultivating any new relationship, it starts and grows through frequent contact; talking, listening, and learning about him. It takes work; you can start slowly and work into it. The important thing is to start.

Free will is a problem for most of us. In today's world, with its focus on emotions, appetites, and desires, your free will prefers to operate without guidance. When you consider a decision that's obedient to God and your rectitude, fear attacks. Maybe you'd have to give up things you like, not have as much fun or success.

Since getting to Heaven is a high priority, you must walk a path that leads to your intended destiny. You don't have to give up free will; life can still be fun, interesting, and satisfying. But your life must be guided by God's values, God's mission.

A relationship with God begins by committing to daily prayer time. Include time for praise, petition, and listening. If time permits, combine it with your Bible study. Don't try too much at first, say 5 to 15 minutes.

Praise is telling God what you think of his infinite love, mercy, and other blessings; and thanking him for what he has done for you and others.

Petition is asking God for your needs and wants. You don't have to ask only for important or holy things, it's okay to throw in a few wants as well. God is a loving Father, and he doesn't mind throwing a chocolate bar your way now and then.

Listening is being attentive to thoughts that might be planted by the Holy Spirit. You can't just accept every thought as coming from God though. They must be tested. Evil likes to interfere. Your appetites and desires plant ideas as well.

It takes a while for God to develop in you the ability to recognize what comes from him. Don't take action on thoughts or direction you receive without confirmation, but keep at it.

Who Is Lord?

In the olden days of kings, queens, and knights, the king sat on his throne and ruled however he pleased. A crucial question will arise as your relationship with God deepens: Who is sitting on your throne? Who is the king of your life? Who will direct your actions and mission? Is it you? Or will it be someone else?

You have several options.

- Evil will tempt you to let emotions, appetites, and desires rule.
- The culture of the world wants you to just go along, go with the

flow, follow whatever is the movement of the day.

- Your own pride will insist there be no outside influences at all. Do whatever you want, whenever you want, with no concern for anyone else.

- Jesus is another option. He offers a new life, freed from the stain of Adam and Eve's sin, and He'll lead you to your intended inheritance.

What you decide will have a major influence in your travels. There is no way you can escape the choosing. The outside influences are relentless. The best choice is obvious, Jesus should be the King, the Lord in your life.

To install him, you must decide to relinquish your own lordship. That's no easy decision. You'll be second in command, but it never means you're a puppet. It means you defer as best you can to input provided by the Holy Spirit in your decisions. In the end, you make the decisions, and you are accountable.

To install Jesus on the throne of your life, first renounce Satan and all of his followers. Then, ask Jesus to be the Lord of your life. Ask him to release more of the Holy Spirit that you received in baptism. It is helpful to praise God that Jesus and the Holy Spirit will be partners with you on your road to Heaven.

Your decision to make Jesus the Lord of your life brings a considerable amount of peace. It opens you to an additional release of the Holy Spirit, bringing many spiritual gifts, including wisdom, faith, gifts of healing, and understanding of the Scriptures. A Brother and Counsellor will be on call to assist you in the many problems you encounter.

Servant Mentality

The servant mentality does not imply being a doormat or an unthinking worker responding to his master in a mechanical fashion. It means an approach to life based on the biblical word *agápe*, meaning God's love.

Jesus uses the words *slave* and *servant* in reference to his *agápe* love for us. The disciples are to serve, not "*lord it over*" (Matt 20:25–28). In biblical days, servants carried sizeable responsibilities, but were always aware of the master's needs, placing his above their own.

A *servant's heart* is aggressive, not waiting for orders, but anticipating, seeking out needs and giving them first priority. Does this suggest a human doormat, someone who obeys without limit or discernment? No. How can that be godly? A servant's heart focuses on *needs*, not *wants*.

Needs are rooted in the very foundation of life; deep, long-term issues that involve the survival, protection, character-building, and community aspects of the individual. They are the keys to releasing life and growth in the beloved. *Wants* are emotional issues, shallow vagaries—driving, powerful urges one moment and all but forgotten the next.

Agápe's application varies depending on the relationship involved. A casual encounter on the street or in the limited responsibilities at work is considerably different than the agápe required in a marriage commitment.

A man of God navigates his way through relationships and levels of responsibility practicing agápe as best he can. It takes a lot of prayer, wisdom from the Holy Spirit, the gift of faith, and time, to develop experience in service of the Lord. It's a lifetime commission, a rich and rewarding life, full of challenges.

Does anyone get it exactly right? Well, we keep trying, and we're making progress. Our Lord's love, peace, wisdom, and forgiveness is always on call.

Grandpa School's out. I congratulate you for your attentiveness and efforts to absorb the presentations. Your grades and graduation certificate will be delivered at judgment.

I pray that God's grace will keep you close to him, and that you remain faithful to your rectitude. I pray, too, that the rest of your life will be a summer vacation. In closing, I leave you with this...

He's alive!!
What are you going to do about God?

Index

About Love 43
Accessible God 13
Angels 16
Bible Study 24
Catholic Christianity 26
Catholic Church 27
Close to God 58
Commandments and Dating 45
Creation's How 3
Discernment of Spirits 33
Don't Get Divorced 51
Emotions 37
Evil's Tactics 17
God's What and Who 5
Integrity 31
Introduction 1
Jesus 25
Judgment 12
Managing the Mind 41
Mankind 9
Marital Mission 52
Marital Tactics 54
Marital Threats 53
Office of the Faithful 30
Original Sin 16
Prime Mover 4
Redeemer Son 19
Regular Discernment 32
Revelation 5
Servant Mentality 60
Sex Overview 39
Submission 11
The New Testament 23
The Old Testament 22
Three Persons, One God 7
Who Is Lord? 59
Your Existence 11

Made in the USA
Columbia, SC
31 July 2018